Big Military Machines

Mary Kate Doman

Enslow Elementary
an imprint of

Enslow Publishers, Inc.
40 Industrial Road
Box 398
Berkeley Heights, NJ 07922
USA

http://www.enslow.com

For Quinn, whose dad flies big military machines.

Enslow Elementary, an imprint of Enslow Publishers, Inc.

Enslow Elementary® is a registered trademark of Enslow Publishers, Inc.

Library of Congress Cataloging-in-Publication Data

Doman, Mary Kate, 1979–
  Big military machines / by Mary Kate Doman.
     p. cm. — (All about big machines)
  Includes index.
  Summary: "Learn how military machines are used every day"—Provided by publisher.
  ISBN 978-0-7660-3932-2
  1. Transportation, Military—Juvenile literature. 2. Vehicles, Military—Juvenile literature. 3. Airplanes, Military—Juvenile literature. 4. Warships—Juvenile literature. I. Title.
  UC270.D66 2012
  355.8—dc23

                        2011014534

Paperback ISBN 978-1-59845-243-3

Printed in the United States of America

052011 Lake Book Manufacturing, Inc., Melrose Park, IL

10 9 8 7 6 5 4 3 2 1

Photo Credits: Cpl. Theodore W. Ritchie, pp. 6–7; Department of Defense, pp. 20–21 U.S. Marine Corps photo by Cpl. Christopher O'Quin, p. 10; U.S. Marine Corps photo by Lance Cpl. Tyler L. Main, pp. 8–9; U.S. Navy photo by Capt. Jaime Quejada/Released, pp. 4–5; U.S. Navy photo by MCS 2nd Class Paul D. Williams/Released, pp. 22–23; U.S. Navy photo by MCS 3rd Class Stephen M. Votaw/Released, pp. title page, 12–13, 14–15; 16–17

Cover Photo: U.S. Navy photo by Mass Communication Specialist 3rd Class Kristin L. Grover/Released

Note to Parents and Teachers

Help pre-readers get a jumpstart on reading. These lively stories introduce simple concepts with repetition of words and short simple sentences. Photos and illustrations fill the pages with color and effectively enhance the text. Free Educator Guides are available for this series at www.enslow.com. Search for the *All About Big Machines* series name.

Contents

Words to Know

aircraft carrier   **helicopter**   **troops**

Big military machines
do big jobs.

Tanks roll.

They roll on the ground.

Jets fly.

They fly fast.

Helicopters lift.

They lift troops.

Ships sail.

They sail in the sea.

Submarines dive.

They dive deep.

Aircraft carriers help.

They help other big military machines travel.

Big military machines carry troops.

They carry troops home.

Big military machines are good at big jobs!

23

Read More

Doeden, Matthew. *Military Helicopters.* Minneapolis, MN: Lerner Publishing Group, 2005.

Newman, Patricia. *Nugget on the Flight Deck.* New York: Walker Books for Young Readers, 2009.

Simons, Lisa M. Bolt. *The Kids' Guide to Military Vehicles.* Minneapolis, MN: Capstone Press, 2009.

Web Sites

Smithsonian Air and Space Museum: Collections—Aircraft
<http://www.nasm.si.edu/> Then click on Collections. Then click on Aircraft.

U.S. Navy: Featured Galleries
<http://www.navy.mil/view_galleries.asp> Then click on Aircraft Carriers.

Index

Guided Reading Level: **C**
Guided Reading Leveling System is based on the guidelines recommended by Fountas and Pinnell.

Word Count: **61**